FROM THE
HEART
OF THE
SPIRIT

NINA AUSTIN

authorHOUSE®

AuthorHouse™
1663 Liberty Drive
Bloomington, IN 47403
www.authorhouse.com
Phone: 1 (800) 839-8640

New International Version (NIV)
Holy Bible, New International Version®, NIV® Copyright
©1973, 1978, 1984, 2011 by Biblica, Inc.® Used by permission. All rights reserved worldwide.

Published by AuthorHouse 03/17/2017

ISBN: 978-1-5246-8373-3 (sc)
ISBN: 978-1-5246-8372-6 (e)

Library of Congress Control Number: 2017903941

Print information available on the last page.

CHAPTER 1

It is with utmost gratitude and humility that I have been inspired to write this book. I never imagined it possible that someone like me, with so little faith, could be touched so deeply by the Spirit of God. The seed of faith was planted in me, as it was in many others, when I was a small child. Growing up as a Catholic girl, I went through all the motions. I attended Mass every day during the week, and missing church on Sunday was never an option. In fact, it was unthinkable.

My dad suffered from the disease of alcoholism and was commonly referred to by my older siblings as a "binge drinker." I was a change-of-life baby, the youngest of four children. My oldest brother was sixteen years old when I was born, and when I was three years old, he enlisted in the air force. My second-oldest brother followed in his footsteps and also enlisted in the air force. I never had any memories of living at home with either of my brothers, and I always wished I would have been born earlier in their lives. I was very proud of their decision to make a career of the military and their service to our country. On one rare occasion, when I was in the third grade, they were able to come home together for a short visit. Much to my surprise, they picked me up from school. Walking down the hall with both of my brothers fully dressed in their military uniforms, and me in the center, was one of the happiest and proudest moments of my life.

My sister was seven years older than I, and I have many happy memories of having an older sister. I was the little sister who resembled a fly at a picnic. I could be quite the nuisance and test her patience. Regardless of that, I felt close to her and have always looked up to her. I knew she held no resentment toward me, because no matter how much I got on her nerves, I always managed to make her laugh. I distinctly remember that because it made me happy that I could make her laugh despite myself. When I was fifteen, she left home and married her high school sweetheart. I missed having my big sister home with me, although I was happy that she was beginning a new chapter in her own life.

When either of my brothers would come home on leave and my sister would stop by for a visit, I would eavesdrop on their quiet conversations with Mom concerning Dad. I did not understand why they would label him an alcoholic. In my eyes, if Dad could hold down a job working in a steel mill, then he certainly shouldn't be placed in the category of an alcoholic. I found their description of my dad's drinking very offensive, and I never hesitated to tell them so. At the time, I knew very little about the disease of alcoholism. To even suggest that he had a problem with alcohol was unacceptable to me. I realize now that I was in denial. My love for my dad and my pity for him turned me in to his best enabler.

Dad was a tall, outspoken man who never minced his words. For those who remember the comedian Carroll O'Connor, who played the role of Archie Bunker, his personality was very much like Dad's. He told you exactly what was on his mind, like it or not. Beneath the surface, he was a kind and caring man, and I loved him with every fiber of my being. I was a daddy's girl for sure.

Mom, on the other hand, was a woman on a mission. She did everything humanly possible to get Dad to stop drinking. This included hiding his shoes and other articles of clothing, to prevent him from leaving the house. He did leave on one occasion wearing his bedroom slippers. Thankfully, he always managed to leave the house fully clothed. I didn't like Mom very much when I was growing up, though. I perceived her as not only an angry woman but a woman who had very little love in her heart for my dad. It was incomprehensible to me why she couldn't just leave him alone to sleep off his intoxication. Since I always felt sorry for him, I would quickly come to his defense. When Dad was not drinking, life seemed normal. There was peace on earth—or at least peace at home.

Christmastime was exceptionally difficult for me as a child. When Mom and Dad would do their Christmas shopping, I felt the anticipation and excitement that most children feel during the Christmas season. I knew St. Nick would stop by, and there would be plenty of gifts under the tree. Unfortunately, by Christmas night, Dad would be drunk, and Mom would sit at the kitchen table and cry. I couldn't understand why Christmas wasn't more about the Christ child and gift giving like I had been taught both at home and at school. I would find myself focusing more on Dad's drinking and Mom's sadness. I struggled with this, and it left me feeling unhappy every year as Christmas evening grew near. It resulted in feelings of not only sadness but confusion.

I remember kneeling by my bed, hands folded in prayer, asking God to please make Dad stop drinking and Mom stop crying and help both of my parents be happy. God never seemed to answer my prayers. I think perhaps it was then I began to question whether God even existed.

Whenever Dad would begin to drink again, I assumed the role of the referee. I would give it my best effort to get between them to try to stop Mom from smacking him when her frustration and anger were out of control. It was always a direct result of his obsession with alcohol. Dad seemed to have no bottom when alcohol was controlling his life.

When he was off on a binge, I would sit on the steps of the front porch, waiting for him to stagger down the street toward our home. He knew how much I loved peanut butter cups (and still do). He would greet me with a smile and a peanut butter cup in each pocket. Then he would plead with me to please keep Mom off his back so he could sleep it off. Dad was not an abusive alcoholic. In fact, when he was under the influence of alcohol, he was like a big teddy bear. I wanted very much to protect him from harm and felt it was my responsibility to do so.

When I became an adult, I began to see Mom from a different perspective. I realized how difficult it was for her to deal with my dad's behavior patterns when he was drinking. She never had the opportunity to attend any support groups to help her cope with people we love who suffer from the untreated disease of alcoholism. She was a stay-at-home mom and never had the desire to drive a car. This made her dependent on my father for almost everything in life. I knew he loved her very much, and when Dad was sober, she changed from the angry wife to the much happier wife, and he was the king of the house. When Dad would become discontented and irritable, I knew it was time to prepare myself for another inevitable bender. When it came to his drinking, he was always predictable.

CHAPTER 2

I attended a Catholic elementary school and was a favorite with the nuns. We lived in a neighborhood where nothing was a secret. The nuns had to be aware of Dad's drinking escapades, and I think perhaps they gave me a little special attention to draw me out of my introverted personality. Many people who had nuns as educators did not share the same experience I did!

When I was in the fourth grade, there was a teacher who needed a ride to a religious bookstore. She asked the class to raise their hands if they thought their parents would be available to give her a ride. No one raised a hand. I'm not sure if I felt sorry for her or if I was trying to be a teacher's pet. I think perhaps it was a little of both. I raised my hand, knowing full well there would be consequences.

When I returned home from school, I told Mom what I had done, and she looked surprised and concerned. She suggested that I go to my room, and when Dad came home from work, she would talk to him on my behalf. He hadn't yet surrendered to his disease, and just because he was not drinking at the time, he was not always a happy camper. I could hear him protest and use some choice language to express his feelings about what I had gotten him into. He agreed to give the nun a ride, but he warned me I was never to volunteer his services again. I went along on the drive to the bookstore. I remember being in the back seat of the car with the nun. We were chatting away, and I was in my glory. I observed the back of my dad's head as he stared at the road ahead, and I caught a glance of a side profile of his not-so-happy face. I knew I was in big trouble. On the trip home, Dad began to make small talk with the nun and seemed to enjoy their conversation. I uttered a sigh of relief.

On three different occasions, she asked for help getting to the bookstore, and even though I received those stern warnings, I continued to raise my hand. Mom just looked at me in disbelief the second time when I returned home to tell her I had done it again. This time, Dad was livid, and I knew it was in my best interest to remain in my room. When I heard him coming up the stairs to give me a second warning, I knew I had really provoked him this time. I found myself, once again, perched in the back seat of the car, heading back to the bookstore. I think the nun suspected Dad wasn't very happy, so I was relieved that she put forth an effort to talk with him on a more personal level and try to get to know him. On the final trip to the bookstore, Dad was starting to soften a little, but he was still resentful that I was volunteering his services without his permission. He often used the words "For Christ's sake." All these years later, I realize it was for Christ's sake! Everything in life really does happen for a reason.

When it came time to enter high school, I wanted to attend a Catholic school. The tuition was high compared to the cost of living, so my parents opted to enroll me in the public-school system. The summer before school began, I was starting to have feelings of doubt and insecurity. Being with the nuns was like a safe haven to me, and I knew it was not going to be an easy transition. I dreaded the first day of high school so much that I considered running away. Since I had no clue where to run to, I decided I had no other choice than to go to school. My attitude was pessimistic, and I felt fear and anxiety.

When the time finally arrived to begin high school, the importance of getting a good education meant nothing to me. I was rebellious and indifferent from day one. I made no attempt to make friends. I was always lost in thought, and I was once again just going through the motions. When I finally decided to attempt to make friends, I was drawn to those who appeared to be like me. I knew that if I was going to keep any friendships, I had to peek my head out of my shell. I assumed the role of leader of the pack. My friends and I spent countless hours in detention and thought we were clever when we managed to elude it.

I also spent many hours in the office under the supervision of the guidance counselor. She was really a very nice woman. She would always smile at me and attempt to get me to open my thoughts to her. I didn't know what was wrong, so I remained silent. I would display my defiant body language and respond, "Well, you're the guidance counselor. Shouldn't you be telling *me* what's wrong?"

She never lost patience with me. She would look up at me while she was doing her paperwork, glasses on her nose, and in her soft voice, she would ask, "What's wrong, honey?"

I wanted very much to cry out to her or just break down and cry, but I concealed those emotions. Her name was Mabel, and my friends loved to tease me and ask how my visits with Mabel were. To keep up my pack leader image, I would reply, "She doesn't bother me. Anything to get out of class was fine with me." I will never forget that kind and compassionate woman, and I know now that she is in a much better place. Despite my attitude, she didn't get upset. She always maintained her composure and managed to keep a smile on her face. Perhaps she was an angel. Anyone who could tolerate my bizarre behavior had to be.

During my final year in high school, I encountered a new friend. Carol was different from any of my other friends. She was a good student, well liked and respected by her peers. When she approached me and began to talk to me, I enjoyed our conversation. She was down to earth and friendly. I felt honored that someone like her would want to have me, of all people, as a friend. We were in two of the same classes, so we walked down the hallway together, chatting nonstop as we went from one class to the next. Some of my other friends would make derogatory comments about Carol, but I chose to ignore them.

I will never forget one day in gym class. We were in the locker room, rushing to get ready for our next class. Carol was a few rows over from me, and I heard her call my name. When I answered, she said she didn't know what was wrong, but she was unable to see anything. I responded that I would be there in a moment. By the time I got to her locker, she was lying on the floor, surrounded by some of the faculty members. We were all gathered around Carol, trying to understand what was happening. We were told we all had to leave the gym immediately. I explained that Carol had been calling for me. I knew the instructions to leave the gym applied to me as well, and there were going to be no exceptions made.

When I arrived at my next class, I could hear the siren of the ambulance. I couldn't get Carol and the vision of her kind and pretty face out of my mind. I learned when I arrived at school the next morning that Carol had died the previous night of a brain aneurysm. I walked around the school that day in a state of disbelief. This couldn't be true.

When I returned home that day, I told my parents what had happened. They tried to console me, but I just wanted to go to my room and be alone. I remember yelling, "God, I don't even believe you are real, but just in case you are, you're a very mean god, and I don't want anything to do with you!" Why would he take the life of a young girl who had so much potential and her whole future ahead of her? I was fixated on the walls as I lay in my bed, and all I could do was continue to stare. When I was finally able to cry, it felt like I would never stop. To this day, when someone loses a friend, Carol still comes to mind. I will always be grateful that I had the opportunity to get to know her and call her a friend.

After Carol's passing, I felt like we had a friendship that was irreplaceable. For a long time after Carol's death, I became a loner. I believed that nobody could ever take Carol's place, but finally, as time passed, I did develop other healthy friendships.

Since I was not attending a Catholic school, my parents enrolled me in religious-education classes on Monday evenings. Not only did I protest but I didn't show up for class most of the time. Sometimes I would make an appearance, but I was only taking up space. I was not open to hearing another word about God, faith, or anything remotely connected to it. For the four years of those classes, I could block out anything I had no interest in, which included everything that was taught in the classes. The only things I enjoyed about the classes—when I did decide to make an appearance—were the occasional pizza parties and just talking with the instructors about anything that came to mind, only if the conversations didn't involve those dreaded discussions about God.

My parents began to receive calls from the parish priest, questioning my whereabouts. When confronted, I would respond by telling them that I didn't like those classes, and it was unfair of them to insist that I go. Confused as I was, I was also very belligerent and displayed typical adolescent behavior.

I recalled what I was told by the nuns in my first few years in elementary school. They said that if you missed church on Sunday and you didn't go to the priest to confess your sins, you would go straight to hell, no stops along the way. My parents had missed church on Sundays, and I remember worrying about that.

What if they died during the week? I couldn't bear the thought, so I asked them if they could miss church on Sunday and that was okay, then why was I being forced to go somewhere I didn't want to be? That made no sense to me whatsoever. The only thing that comment got me was a stern look and a reminder that they weren't going to tolerate any more phone calls from the parish priest due to my lack of attendance.

I somehow managed to graduate high school. How I did it remains a mystery. I would lug my backpack home every night, heavily weighted down with books, and they would remain in a chair untouched. My parents would question me, and I was never truthful. I would tell them I had completed all my assignments while I was at school. If I had been a believer, the fact that I could graduate would have fallen in to the category of a miracle. My feelings of hopelessness, apprehension, and anger were like a cancer, eating away at my soul.

CHAPTER 3

Following graduation, I still doubted the existence of God and was on a path that led me to a place of darkness and despair. All my negative thoughts about life in general held me hostage in a state of hopelessness. I convinced myself this was my destiny, and I held no hope that life would ever change.

My pride kept me from reaching out and asking for help. I didn't want to be labeled the biggest nut on the family tree. Although at the time I felt like I was indeed! It is amazing how, when I lived in my own little world, consumed with doubt and fear, my mind still gave me options. If things got bad enough that I couldn't survive life as I knew it, I could always swallow my pride and ask for help. Any hopeful thoughts always seemed to be quickly dismissed with more thoughts of doom and gloom.

The closest connection I had to feeling happiness was knowing that I loved my parents and all my family near and far. I didn't want to trouble them with my problems, although I know now if I had reached out for help, they would have tried their best to help me find my way out of the darkness. I come from a very large family, and we are scattered all over the United States. Although they are far away in distance, they have always remained close at heart.

I had no idea how to come to terms with my innermost feelings. After all, this was my destiny. I was trapped in a web of sadness, and I believed there was no way out. I tried blaming everything on my experiences as a small child, with the chaos and discontent taking place. I felt that wasn't the problem because all families go through hard times. As depressed as I was, I never once considered ending what appeared to me to be a meaningless existence. Besides, I was too nosy. I wanted to stick around and see what was going to happen next. Maybe there was a happiness fairy that would drop some dust on my head and poof! I would find happiness.

Some positive changes began to happen in my parents' lives. There was a man named Gene who would come to our home. He was the one person who could sit quietly and talk with my mom, and she seemed calm and peaceful. When Gene was there, I felt calm also. Then he would take my dad to a drug and alcohol rehab. I had mixed emotions. I was relieved that the arguing would stop but sad that Dad was leaving. I found out later that Gene was a member of Alcoholics Anonymous. My Dad had finally surrendered to his disease. It didn't happen overnight. Gene came to our home several times, and Dad would be off again to the rehab. After several attempts, he finally got sober and stayed sober. Years later, I wanted to find Gene to thank him. I learned that he had passed away. He will always have a place in my heart, that special place where gratitude resides.

CHAPTER 4

In the late 1970s, Dad developed problems with his heart. At first it appeared hopeful that medication would solve the problem. I had my driver's license by then, and Mom and I would take him to his doctor appointments. He had mellowed with age, and I could sense his inner peace. I noticed how concerned Mom was when his health began to decline. The love that I thought Mom never had for Dad was there and couldn't have been more obvious. Observing their affection for one another made me realize how wrong I was when I doubted her love for him. I realized how much I loved them both.

Dad's heart problems became worse, and he had to be hospitalized several times. It became apparent that his final days on earth were drawing near. I wanted to be strong for my mom. The realization that someone we love is approaching the end of their life is among the most painful emotions we experience and the most difficult to conceal. I was slowly learning that suppressing my emotions was unhealthy, and I had to find a way to accept the inevitable.

Mom was much stronger than I was, and she had discovered ways to cope with difficult times. She always tried to remain positive and find things to be cheerful about. She said on more than one occasion, "Worry is like interest paid on a debt before the debt is due." When I shared with Mom that I wanted to be strong for her, she suggested that I pray. I knew Mom believed in prayer. In one of our mother-daughter talks, she told me that when Dad was drinking and she felt distraught, she would pray and ask God for help. I didn't want to let her know how I felt about God and prayer, because I feared I would take away her faith. I didn't realize then that faith is a gift from God that no one can take away. I was afraid to pray. I didn't want to take the risk of having any more unanswered prayers from a God who, if he did exist, seemed distant and unreachable.

Prior to Dad's last visit to the hospital, my family was planning a reunion at Lake of the Ozarks in Missouri. My sister was unable to attend, and Mom wanted to stay home to be near Dad. I did not want to leave him, but my brothers felt it would be a good diversion to get my mind off Dad's illness and spend some time with the rest of the family. I was wavering because I really wanted to see all the family, but I didn't want to leave him. They finally convinced me to join them.

When I walked into Dad's hospital room to tell him I would be leaving for a week, I wasn't surprised to see two nuns sitting by his bed, praying with him. I got to his bedside just in time to hear the end of their prayer. I recalled when I had assigned him the job of the taxi driver for the nun in my elementary years. I knew that he believed it was for Christ's sake. It brought a smile to my face.

When I sat down on the bed next to Dad and we discussed the family reunion, the tears began to flow. When I told him I didn't want to leave him, he affectionately stroked the side of my face with the palm of his hand. He said he would be fine, and he wanted me to go and have a good time. He had asked me twice during our visit when I would be returning home. I told him I would be back the following Friday. I was concerned because he was beginning to lose his appetite. I convinced him to let me help him sip on an energy drink. Life had come full circle. Before I left his hospital room, I gave him a hug and a kiss on the cheek. As I approached the door, I felt compelled to turn around to say good-bye again. He looked at me with bright eyes and a little smile on his face and said it was no wonder he loved me so much. I responded, "I love you too, Dad."

During my time spent with family, we enjoyed being together. Dad came to mind often, but I remembered his words that he wanted me to enjoy myself. When the end of the reunion approached, I was reminded by the family that we had a special day coming up on Friday—a birthday to celebrate. I tried to call both the hospital and home so Dad would be aware that I would be returning home a day later than planned, but I was unable to reach anyone.

On the long drive, back home on Saturday, we pulled the car over. I wanted to call home again. When my sister answered the phone, I could tell by the sound of her voice that she had been crying. Dad loved all his children, and we all loved him. She had the unpleasant task of telling me that our dad had passed away on Saturday morning.

She and my mom were there with Dad for his last days. They were painful days for Dad, and I don't know if I would have been able to watch him suffer. My brothers and their wives had already been notified of Dad's passing. They arrived back in their hometown from the reunion shortly before I did. I was grief-stricken, but knowing that we were all there for Mom and for one another helped to ease our sorrow. For a long time, I blamed myself that I never made it home by Friday. I felt like Dad tried to wait for me, although I knew for some reason it just wasn't meant to be. When I first lost Dad, I felt like a small part of my heart died with him. When I think about Dad today, my happy memories far outweigh my grief. I am grateful for our last words to one another—such a beautiful and cherished memory.

CHAPTER 5

Life went on, and I noticed that almost everyone around me appeared to be happy. I was still searching for answers, and I arrived at the conclusion that the nuns weren't honest with me. Maybe thoughts of God were just happy thoughts to explain the existence of mankind. Perhaps God didn't create man; maybe man created God. Even though my overactive mind created that thought, strangely, I felt the urge to reject it.

I continued to spend a lot of time lost in more thoughts of negativity and doubt. Spending my time in thought was an unhealthy obsession and solved nothing. I realized that I had now assumed the role of my own psychologist. If you are questioning your sanity and you spend too much time in your head, you will very likely convince yourself that you are a unique kind of crazy!

My mom began asking why I was spending so much time alone and why I always looked so sad. She tried to talk to me, and I would just shake my head and say nothing was wrong; I was fine. I wanted desperately for her to believe me. When she didn't look convinced, I started to cry. When I saw the look of bewilderment on her face, I told her I had a crush on a guy I had met before graduation and I was upset because he didn't appear to be interested in me. I wanted to give her a reason that was believable. Even though that was a façade, it seemed to work. It really intensified my sadness to see her so concerned. I finally decided to tell her a silly joke I had heard, and we both laughed. That was a relief because I didn't want to cause her any further unhappiness. I knew how much she missed my dad; we both did.

I continued to isolate myself. My distorted thinking only fueled my desire to stay within myself. I felt if I built a wall around myself, I wouldn't have to participate in life with the rest of the world. At least that way I could conceal my unhappiness and keep my pride intact. Sadly, society still places that stigma on people who, for whatever reason, think differently than others. I didn't want to be labeled as unstable or incapable of managing my own life, even though I knew deep inside that it was not a normal way to live. It took a lot of time, as the years passed, to try to chip away at that wall and get to the root of the problem.

I began having flashbacks of kneeling by my bed, and those same feelings erupted. If God was real, he would have helped me and wouldn't have ignored me when I begged him for help. He wouldn't have taken my dad or such a special friend away, and he certainly wouldn't have made me so miserable. Every time I heard others discussing their faith, I wanted to challenge their beliefs and tell them how I felt, but I remained quiet. The hole in my soul was becoming increasingly larger. The cancer was growing.

CHAPTER 6

Two weeks after graduating from high school, I began what was to become my career job. My sister had called me and told me the company that she worked for was hiring. I said yes, I was interested. I worked in communications, and I liked the job. It was a great diversion from sitting around, dwelling on the purpose of life and trying to solve the problems of the world. I knew that to keep that job, I had to be cooperative and willing to work as a team with my coworkers. The job gave me motivation, and I took pride in my efforts to work hard and be a good employee.

I began to make friends at work and would join them during breaks. Since I was talking constantly to clients, I could see I had come a long way. I was gradually starting to become less introverted, and I wanted to join in on their conversations. There were certain friends who loved to talk about their places of worship and their involvement in their community of believers. One person seemed obsessed with the idea. I wished they would stop with all the God talk and discuss something I could join in on.

One day, I was approached by my boss, who informed me that a new employee would be joining me at my desk, to observe and learn the job requirements. I had no objection to that and hoped I would be of help to him as he received his on-the-job training. He appeared to be a nice man and was busy taking notes. When we had a lull in the incoming call volume, we had the opportunity to get to know a little about one another. He said he had just transferred to my hometown from Iowa. He talked with me about his family. He was very pleasant, and he explained that this was only a part-time job for him. His main and most preferred job was as a Baptist minister in a small church in my hometown in Pennsylvania. Great, just what I needed. I was waiting to see how long it would take before he started asking me questions. I assumed those questions would eventually lead to his asking me about my beliefs. I thought I had lucked out and discovered he was not going to mix work with religion. Or so I thought!

When he accompanied me to the break room, I noticed he was casually easing into the conversation. He asked about my family, and then he caught me off guard. He threw me quite a curve ball, and I forgot to duck. He boldly announced that he had been saved. It wasn't the first time I had heard that word, and I detested it! I told him I had not been saved. Thankfully, he couldn't read my mind.

From that day forward, he never missed an opportunity to tell me I could be saved too. I resented this man because I wondered what made him so special that he had received this so-called gift of salvation. For the first time, I could finally find a word to describe my lack of faith. Without a shadow of doubt, I was an agnostic. The one thing that "saved" him from my disbelief was his smile. Those conversations annoyed me, but since smiles are infectious, I decided to just let him say what he felt he needed to say, and I didn't become angry with him. I did feel annoyed because I felt empty inside with a void that remained unfulfilled.

On another occasion at work, I looked up, and he was standing near my desk. He shared with me that he had been transferred back to Iowa and had been offered a position as a minister at a large church in his hometown. His dream of being able to minister once again in his hometown had finally come true. On his last day of work, he approached me again to say good-bye and tell me he would be praying for me. I smiled back at him and wished him good luck. As far as his comment about praying for me, I thought to myself, *Good luck with that!* I knew I would miss this man, but I was not going to miss his constant preaching to me.

After the minister left, I continued to encounter coworkers who would discuss God by sharing their constant annoying chatter. My resentment was multiplying. I started having flashbacks again and feeling that if there was a God, he surely never cared about me, so why should I waste my time trying to grasp the concept of believing in him, because he probably didn't even exist. I still was unable to connect my disbelief in God as the source of my troubled soul. It was much easier to put him completely out of my thoughts. My resentment toward those who had faith or were pretending to was getting to the point that I felt like a pot of hot water that was about to boil over. If that pot were to reach its boiling point, it wasn't going to be a pretty sight! I was on the verge of unleashing my ill feelings on whoever happened to be at the receiving end of my frustration and irritation. That never happened, and I believe, because I never lost the love my heart could hold, that I tried to defeat the disturbing battle taking place within me.

CHAPTER 7

I married in my mid-twenties, and my husband and I opted for a church wedding. The only sense that I could make of that decision was that I knew I was not breaking family tradition by having a wedding ceremony in the Catholic church. We were in love; however, having the marriage blessed in a church was not something I felt had any significance. Neither of us attended church at the time. Since we were preparing to be married in a Catholic church, we were required to take classes. We agreed that if we were to have children, we would raise them in the Catholic faith.

We had two children during that marriage. I loved the excitement and anticipation of giving birth. My nose was constantly in a book so I could learn how big our babies were during each trimester of the pregnancies. I loved being a mom, and my husband was a good dad. We tried our best to be good parents. We wanted to pass on the love to them that we had received throughout our childhood. I think all of us have unhappy circumstances that take place during our childhood. I believe it's never too late to have a happy childhood. It's being able to let go of the unhappy memories that can never be changed and cherishing the good memories that will always remain with us.

When our kids were old enough to start school, my husband and I made the decision to send them to a public school. We enrolled them in religious-education classes. I hoped that what I myself was lacking they could possibly find. I even went out and bought a children's bible. When I would read to them, I felt like I was reading them a fairytale book rather than the Word of God. They didn't seem to mind the religious-education classes in their elementary years. In their high school years, they were a lot like their mom. It was not their favorite place to be.

As we raised our family, we encountered the problems that are a normal part of parenthood. Family life is not always smooth sailing. There was the occasional problem of sibling rivalry, the busyness and chaos of getting the kids to their extracurricular activities, and all those things that are common in the average American family. Sometimes their dad and I did not see eye to eye on things, and we weren't always able to hide this from our children and set a good example. For the most part, we were a family who loved one another and managed to work through most of the problems that all families experience.

Even though the bond of family love was there, days came when we just needed time alone and a little break from family life. Just daydreaming about getting some of the other moms together, renting a van, and just going somewhere for a few days to take a break from the child-rearing years helped to keep me going. Sometimes fantasy daydreaming isn't such a bad thing. However, I never wanted my kids to see my picture along with "mom missing" on a milk carton!

When it was time to enroll our children in the high school's religious-education classes, I found myself in a very awkward, uncomfortable position. There was a very feisty little nun sitting behind the registration desk. She loudly announced that they were in dire need of parent volunteers to teach the elementary classes. I tried to avoid making eye contact with her. Suddenly she called me by name and asked if I would be willing to be a volunteer teacher. When I attempted to explain to her that I had no experience as a teacher and it was not something I was interested in doing, it became quite clear to me that "no" was not an acceptable answer. I agreed, based mostly on guilt, to give it a try. After all, since I was a parent and they had to rely on the parents as teachers, I felt it wasn't unfair of her to ask. The nun seemed relieved, and she smiled—just like the guidance counselor and the Baptist minister.

They didn't have cell phones back then, and as I was driving home, I found myself talking out loud to myself. I said, "Oh my God," and that was not a prayer. I am certain that if anyone was driving past my car and observed me talking to myself, they would have thought I was crazy. What had I gotten myself into, and how was I going to get myself out of this predicament?

Shortly after I agreed to be a volunteer teacher, I was summoned to the religious-education office for a training session. A lot of emphasis was placed on the importance of learning each child's name. It would make them feel special and cared about. Just like adults, we notice when someone takes the time to remember our name. I was assigned to the second grade. That should be easy enough! I would be able to fake my way through these classes and possibly pull this teaching assignment off. I was equipped with a lesson book, and once again I was toting a children's bible. I knew there was no looking back, since I had made this commitment. I also knew I had no choice but to move forward and try to do what was asked of me. But how could I possibly do this when I didn't believe? Life was becoming interesting, to say the least.

CHAPTER 8

When I tried to prepare myself for these classes, I looked at the first lesson plan and began to feel overwhelmed. I put the book aside and went back later to look at it again. With pen and paper in hand, I began to write. I worked very hard on that lesson plan, and I felt a sense of accomplishment. I had a glimmer of hope that that I could make these classes interesting, and I had increasing hope that I could make it through the year and pretend to be a believer.

Even though I loved being a wife and mother, maybe there was more to life that was to be revealed. I was enthusiastic yet nervous about the first class. That was quite a shift in attitude from the direction I was originally headed. Although there was something within me that was beginning to change, it was a subtle transformation. It felt like a dim light, like the lights you use during a power outage. I was unaware of where this light would lead me, but I knew I was open to following this new path.

It wasn't about my life anymore. That calls to mind the book written by Rick Warren, *The Purpose-Driven Life*. In the beginning of that book, it says, "It's not about me." I embraced that truth because I knew there was more that I was meant to do in life. There was a powerful force inside of me. I had yet to discover the source of that power, which was pretty mind-boggling! I waited in anxious anticipation for the first day of class to arrive. At times, I would catch myself feeling doubtful again. I was slowly learning to clear my mind of any negativity. It was a good beginning.

The first day of class was chaotic, to say the least. Those little children were rambunctious, to put it mildly. I explained to them the importance of having respect for me as their teacher and for one another. Much to my surprise, most of them listened. I began to look around the room, and the thought came to mind that possibly they were just as anxious and unsure about the class as their teacher was. I learned a few of their names and observed their faces light up as I called them by name.

I still wasn't sure if I could convince these children that there was a God who loved them. You certainly can't convince anyone of something that you are unsure of and constantly questioning yourself. Those little children touched my heart in a way I couldn't quite put into words. I was nowhere close to making a commitment to God, but at that moment, I did make a commitment to those little ones. I didn't want to let them down. I wasn't as far away as I thought from believing that God was with me, guiding me every step of the way. For that, I will always be filled with humility and gratitude.

After each child shared a little about him- or herself, I was amazed at how smart and attentive they were. They talked about their parents, siblings, pets, and anything that came to their minds. It helped me to get to know them, and I began to feel more relaxed. The trust and innocence of a child is remarkable. It inspired me and gave me incentive to continue. Halfway through the class, we had a question-and-answer period. I practiced my deep breathing to try to conquer the fear that they may ask me a question I would not be able to answer. I simply reverted to what the nuns had taught me. I believed it at the time, so hopefully they would believe it too. As I pondered the questions they were asking, I began to reflect on what I was about to tell them. Just maybe the answers I was giving them were true. The doubt I was still feeling was slowly being overshadowed by a ray of hope. I was still skeptical, but as long as they didn't pick up on that, all was well. Little did they know their teacher was learning to keep an open mind. I was beginning to have some clarity, and I could realize the change within me was not coming *from* me. It was coming from a very powerful force within.

All the parent volunteers were instructed to accompany each child to the cafeteria, to be met by their parents at the end of each class. It was a very large church with several classrooms, and we were forewarned that for each child's safety, the children were to walk, not run. Getting these little ones to follow instructions was a challenge and a true test of patience. When my class was dismissed, one of the eighth-grade girls, tall for her age, came barreling around the corner, and we had a head-on collision. I literally saw stars! I surely wasn't anticipating a nosebleed on the first day of class. I could see that this child was okay and was just as shocked as I. Agitated as I was, I could see by her facial expressions that she too was shocked about what had happened. She apologized, and I knew she was sorry. She learned to follow instructions, and I learned to be aware of those who didn't!

After that first class, when I returned to the classroom, I took some time in the quiet of the moment to reflect. Things went well (aside from the nosebleed) and I felt an inner peace. I was quite surprised that I had used phrases like, "You are all children of God," and "God loves you," and that those statements didn't cause inner turmoil. That was puzzling to me. I felt like I was living in the moment and appreciating it—something that was unfamiliar to me. I realized it wasn't some strange coincidence that when I was asked to help with these classes, I agreed to do so. Life was beginning to change, and I was experiencing an uplifting peace of mind. I was enthusiastic to return home and tell my husband and children how well the class had gone.

CHAPTER 9

As the school year progressed, my enthusiasm increased. I loved the idea of getting the kids involved in special projects. When I shared this plan, I was excited to watch their curiosity mount. I didn't want these classes to be monotonous for them, and I knew they were eager to learn what this special project would entail. Perhaps I had spoken too soon! I wanted to talk with them about their new project, but it was equally important to finish their next lesson. It was a joy to share in their enthusiasm, but it took a little time and patience to get them to settle down. After I got the class under control again, I promised them that if they finished their lesson for the week and time allowed, we would discuss their new project.

I did find time to explain that they would be able to start their project the following week and they could work together to choose a name to describe it. They waited enthusiastically. I don't know who was more excited about this new endeavor, them or me. We are all God's children, and I was capable of sharing with all the children what I had been taught when I was their age. Those thoughts that were placed in my mind were not of my making. Even though I had been angry and resentful toward God and other believers, through grace I could put those feelings aside. To observe the joy in the eyes of a young child is an amazing and humbling experience—precious moments in the eyes of a loving God.

At the next class, I explained to the children that they would be drawing hearts. Their hearts would be going to a nursing home, and I explained further that often, the nursing home's patients don't have a lot of family to visit them. These hearts would help to brighten their day. Each child was given the name of a new friend in the nursing home. The names they chose for their project were priceless. Some were clever, and some were humorous. They came up with ideas like "Smart Hearts," "Old People's Hearts," and the best one of all: "Hope Your Heart Keeps Beating." That child had put a lot of thought into that title, and I had to put forth a serious effort not to laugh. With a little help from their teacher, they all raised their hands in agreement to name their project "Hearts Full of Love."

There was a sweet little boy named Matthew in the class. I had observed that he would ask at least twice during the one-hour class to use the restroom. I suspected that Matthew was struggling with hyperactivity. I decided to take him outside of the classroom and talk with him. When I asked Matthew if he really had to use the restroom or if he was restless and having trouble sitting still, he just shrugged his shoulders to indicate he really didn't know. I saw a reflection of myself in that sweet little child, and when I asked if I could give him a hug, he nodded. I thought Matthew would never let go. To feel compassion and love for another person, whether it's a little person or an adult, is such a blessing. Unfortunately, because of the world we live in today, just giving a child a hug can cause your motives to be questioned. I will never forget that hug, nor will I ever forget little Matthew. I knew that we both needed a hug, and it has become a cherished memory.

Since Matthew indicated that now he really did need to use the restroom, when I returned to the class, I mentioned that Matthew was having a hard day, and perhaps they could all show him a little extra kindness. When the class went to the back of the room to the art table to begin drawing their hearts, I smiled as I watched several of the other kids gather around Matthew to help him draw his heart. That powerful source felt like it was extending to all those children. It was a serene and hopeful feeling. The love in the classroom that day was exceptional. The messages those little ones wrote in their hearts were chosen with thoughtfulness and care. Some wrote *I love you*, and others wrote *God loves you!* They all actively participated in the project, and it was a pleasure to watch. Another child drew a picture of his dog and wanted his friend in the nursing home to know that if they were ever lonely, they could look at his pet, and he hoped it would make them feel happy and never lonely.

That evening, I took all the hearts they had drawn home with me to look them over again. Their misspelled words were funny, and there was absolutely nothing I wanted to change. That was where they were in their learning process for second grade, and I hoped the nursing-home patients would enjoy the hearts as much as I did.

I had become close friends with another of the parent volunteer teachers. To this day, we have remained friends. Diane is one of the most creative people I have ever known. We would discuss how our classes were going, and some of the ideas she came up with to make learning fun were incredible. Since each child was given the opportunity to become familiar with the Ten Commandments and other Scripture-related words of importance that were part of the lesson plans, she created the idea of "disciple dollars." Each child would be given a disciple dollar when he or she learned something new. At the end of the school year, she planned to have them bring in their old toys. The disciple dollars would be spent buying each other's used toys.

We were discussing this in the office, and the director of religious education overheard our conversation. Judging by the look on her face, we both knew she wasn't too thrilled about that idea. She didn't think bribing the children was a very good plan. We managed to convince her that it wasn't bribing them; it was giving them incentive to learn. She was hesitant but finally reluctantly agreed. We made sure each child would have plenty of disciple dollars to spend when the school year came to an end. When she walked away, we exchanged smiles, and a high-five was in order!

CHAPTER 10

When I went home at night, I began to feel a strong urge to give prayer a chance. I was feeling emotions that were unfamiliar to me, but in a strange, unexplainable way, they felt right. Once again, I believe my decision was encouraged by the Spirit within me that was helping me to overcome my past resentments. I started to look at my husband and my children, and I was seeing things in a much brighter light. I always knew I loved them, but through the grace of God, I became able to connect love to him. The God I thought never cared enough to answer my prayers as a child was with me, and I wanted to talk with him. I wasn't filled with remorse or shame; I was filled with the peace that surpasses all human understanding, the peace that I believed came only from him. It was like waking up from a long slumber and saying, "Hello, God, and thank you for opening my eyes."

My conversations with God were short, and as time passed, they came at the most unexpected times. I believed in my heart that he heard my prayers. All those years ago, when I didn't believe he heard my cry for help, I knew I was wrong. He did hear me. He hears all our prayers.

Since I was no longer feeling anger toward God and I was starting to look forward to my talks with Him, I felt inspired to end each class with a prayer circle. We would join hands, and I explained to the class that we were calling it a prayer circle because a circle has no end, and we could always talk to God because his love for us has no end. When we held hands in our circle, I made sure the children knew that if they couldn't think of anything they wanted to pray about, that was okay too. I hoped they would pray because they wanted to, not because they felt it was a requirement. One of the little girls wanted to pray for her grandma who had cancer. Another child announced that his dog had been throwing up that morning and he wanted to pray for him. One of the other boys quipped that we probably shouldn't be praying for dogs. I responded, "Sure we can." After all, our animals are all part of the Lord's creation, and we prayed that his dog would feel better.

We continued to form our prayer circle at the end of each class. One day when we held hands, I noticed that one of the girls looked unhappy and appeared hesitant. She was one of the most active little prayer warriors in the class. When I looked at her and smiled, she loudly and confidently announced that she wanted to pray for her goldfish, "Oliver," who had died that morning. Not one child laughed. We asked God to help her not to feel so sad. The love and sincerity of a child, whether it be for families, classmates, or pets, is so precious that it really tugs on your heartstrings!

On the last day of class, I asked the children to draw a picture of something that was special to them that they learned in the class and what they enjoyed the most. I wanted to have memories to look back on. One of the children drew a picture of the host, which represents the body of Christ. Next to the host, he wrote the words "good food for my soul." I was unaware of telling him that, but he was right. It is soul food. Another child drew a picture of a boy, and next to that he wrote, "in trouble, out of trouble." I suspected he was referring to himself. Upon further investigation, I discovered he was drawing a picture of the Prodigal Son. I even turned up in some of their pictures. One of the little girls who had a habit of talking out of turn drew a sad face, and next to it was a smiling face with a picture of me. She wrote, "Good Girl, and I love you." That really touched my heart, and I gave her a hug and reassured her that she was a good little girl.

All the teachers agreed it would be nice to have a party the last day of the school year. We celebrated with food and drinks, and things got a little crazy. What happened to my little angels? They were chasing each other all around the classroom. When you have twenty-one children in a class and they are chasing each other all over, *crazy* describes the situation perfectly. They had finally started to settle down, so these little angels had recovered their wings. After all, even as adults, we occasionally lose our wings. I loved every hug I received and every hug I gave in return as they left the classroom. Without a doubt, I would never forget these children who were placed by God in my care. When class came to an end and they were all lined up and ready to go home, I realized how much I would miss them.

When I went to the office to turn in the lesson book and the children's bible, I was greeted with a smile from the feisty little nun—another reminder of the same smile I received from the guidance counselor and the Baptist minister. I knew exactly what she was going to ask me. I remained a volunteer teacher for the next five years. I had already begun my journey from darkness to light. That word, "saved," that I detested so much had begun to take on a different meaning, and it was no longer invasive or bothersome to me. My world of darkness was leading me in to the light of a loving and forgiving God!

CHAPTER 11

Following the summer of the first year of class, my husband, my children, and I began to attend church on a regular basis. He had made the decision to convert to Catholicism. Things were going well, and I was happy that he too had begun his spiritual journey. I loved to sing along with the congregation at church. I would get so enthusiastic my husband and kids had already begun to leave their seats as the Mass was ending. I never even noticed they had left, because I was busy singing away. They would wait for me at the back of the church with big smiles on their faces. It became a family joke we often laughed about. My singing voice left a lot to be desired, but when I was singing songs of praise and worship, it never mattered. Music has a way of opening your heart and awakening your soul.

I wanted the four of us to pray together as a family at home. On the few occasions we did pray together, I hoped we would be creating a special and permanent bond. We weren't always on the same page when prayer was suggested, and I didn't want to appear self-righteous or holier than thou and push anyone away. I knew that feeling all too well. Besides, I was in the beginning stages of my own walk with God. I did ask God during my talks with him to bring all four of us closer together as a family. How often have we heard it said that the family that prays together stays together? I don't believe that is just a rhyming phrase. I know and believe that prayer is a powerful source of communication that keeps us focused on our Creator and brings us all closer together.

Later in life, some problems arose in our marriage, and we were both at fault. We sought marriage counseling and other means of resolving our differences, but the marriage of twenty-one years ended in divorce. It was a difficult time for both of us. Our divorce also took a toll on our children. Children of divorced parents often feel angry. Sometimes their anger is directed at one of the parents and sometimes both. Regardless, as parents, you never stop loving your children. We are both very proud of our children, who are now adults with children of their own. They eventually adjusted to the fact that their parents could no longer stay together, but it was just as difficult for them as it was for us when the marriage failed.

I did not want to go through the process of an annulment, and I decided to attend another Christian church that had a recovery group for those trying to cope with divorce. I later learned that my former husband was attending a divorce support group in the Catholic church. I was happy that he too was reaching out for help to recover from the pain of divorce.

Even though I was reaching out for help, I still was carrying around a lot of guilt for the part I played in the marriage ending. My parents were married for fifty-five years. They had struggles in their marriage, but they stayed together. Why was I unable to do my part to make the marriage survive? I began to feel unworthy of God's love. I was beginning to build another wall. I stopped praying as often as I once had. I struggled to forgive myself. The wall I was starting to form was preventing me from feeling God's forgiveness. I was aware that my spiritual growth was stagnant. I felt like I had placed myself in wet cement. I couldn't move backward or forward. I was just stuck in the same place, unable to move on.

I talked to one of the counselors at the divorce recovery group, and she helped me immensely to realize that if we can't forgive ourselves then we are subconsciously separating ourselves from experiencing the grace of God's forgiveness. When I tried to find my way back to God, it was a slow process. I did find comfort in believing that he had never left me. After a lot of tears and soul searching, I was finally able to experience the freedom that comes with acceptance. I was ready to let go of the past and place myself in the presence of our patient, loving God.

CHAPTER 12

Three months following the dissolution of my first marriage, I received some startling news. Like so many other women, I was diagnosed with breast cancer. My prognosis, after completion of the necessary testing, indicated that things weren't looking good. It appeared to be a fast-growing tumor. The medical team determined that they would need to take immediate action to prevent this invasive tumor from spreading. I was beside myself. My family and friends all reached out to me with uplifting words of encouragement and hope. They assured me that they would be praying for me.

Even though I was no longer attending the Catholic church, I had many good Christian friends who were. There was a Catholic priest I had gotten to know well, but I hadn't seen him in a couple of years. He came to mind, and I decided to give him a call. When we spoke, I shared the news with him that I had developed cancer. I commented that I believed I should pray for God's will be done. I was surprised by his quick and adamant response. He replied, "No! You pray for God to heal you." I knew that he would be praying and that I would be taking his advice! God puts people in our lives at the exact moment they are meant to be there. So often I can hear Christ in the voice of others and see a glimpse of him in their acts of kindness and compassion.

Following two surgeries and chemotherapy, I was given the good news that my cancer was in remission and they didn't anticipate a reoccurrence. It was twenty years in 2016 that I have been breast cancer free. I was once again aware that God had given me another blessing. At first, I would find myself wondering why I was so blessed to survive cancer when so many others are not. I stopped trying to understand that, because I never will. If I remain grateful, then no questions need be asked. I accepted that it was God's will for me to live, just as I hope to accept when my time on this earth comes to an end. I have always said that I came into this world kicking and screaming and I may leave this world the same way. One never knows until that time comes. Hope and trust in God's plan for us gives us inner peace and serenity. That peace, he tells us, surpasses all human understanding. Today I don't try to understand God. I do trust, though, that no matter what happens in this life, God is in control.

I haven't overcome all my fears; we all have moments of fear. I personally believe that is why the words *fear not* or *do not be afraid* appear approximately 365 times in the Bible. I am not a biblical scholar, so if you're wondering where I came up with that interesting trivia, I Googled it! I have heard it said many times that fear and faith cannot coexist. I personally have a different opinion about that statement. What I do with my fear strengthens my faith. If I pray about it, then I feel closer to Christ, and he calms my fears.

I, like many others, had a fear of flying. When I placed my hope and trust in God, I could conquer that fear. The "miracle on the Hudson," for instance, left us all in awe of God's ability to do what seems to be the impossible. He was with that pilot that day. I believe in miracles. He is with all of us when we hold on to the hope that only he can provide. Miracles aren't always found in the profound things that happen in life. Life itself is a miracle. In the beauty of the universe we find ourselves. It increases my awareness that we aren't just inhabitants of this world. We are all miracles. We are all spiritual beings in the form of a human body; another beautiful gift from our Creator. It is how we connect to God that defines our spirituality.

I have learned that through Christ, all things are possible. If I keep his infinite love as the center of my life, then my faith continues to grow and my love for him deepens.

CHAPTER 13

In the four years following the divorce, I had made up my mind that I would never remarry. I had feared that another marriage would fail. I dated on occasion, but all my relationships were based solely on friendship. Little did I know that God would place a man in my life who would want to take our friendship to another level.

When I met the man, who was to become my husband, I knew something different was beginning to happen. I loved so much about him. I felt comfortable talking with him, and I felt like I had known him forever. I loved the way his eyes sparkled and how he noticed even the smallest of things. What I was most attracted to was his loving, kindred spirit. He was not only a godly man; he was and still is a man who lives his faith.

On our spiritual journey, together, he has been an inspiration to me. In moments when I am grouchy or short with him, he rarely gets upset with me. He has taught me by example to be slower to anger and even quicker to forgive and to keep moving forward.

I don't know if there is any such thing as a perfect marriage, but I do know that as we continue our lives together, we remember those words we said to one another when we exchanged our marriage vows. We vowed to love one another as God has loved us. Through praying with and for one another, we have been blessed with faith to believe that our marriage will not fail. Matthew 19:6 tells us, "So, then they are no longer two but one flesh; therefore, what God has brought together, let no man separate."

Our faith journey has not been without trials and tribulations. I believe that is God's way of keeping us on our toes. The real test of faith is how we react when life gives us difficult situations. If I forget to pray, my troubles intensify. We are responsible for how we react, but God is always the one who patiently waits for us to bring our troubles to him. I have learned the importance of letting go and letting God! It is a lifelong learning process of asking God for help.

CHAPTER 14

Mom lived twelve years after Dad passed. She was a very determined, independent woman and a constant inspiration to me. She had a way of saying and doing things that made me laugh. The fact that she wasn't aware of how humorous she was made her even funnier. A couple of times on our weekly trips to the grocery store, she would walk off with someone else's cart. She would get a couple of aisles away and still wasn't aware of what she had done. I didn't always notice, because I was shopping also. Then she would glance at her cart, look at me with her big brown eyes, and say, "Now why did you put that in my cart?"

I would say, "Mom, that's not your cart." Then we would share in the laughter.

When I would ask Mom to babysit, there was never a dull moment. My children could be "challenging" at times. When they were being mischievous, she would keep the yardstick close by, just to remind them that they had better behave themselves. When I would pick them up from Grandma's house, I would ask if they were on their best behavior. They would be in the back seat of the car and giggle as they admitted that their grandma had the yardstick out again! Mom had seventeen grandchildren and several great-grandchildren, and she loved them all. Since only two of them resided permanently in Pennsylvania, my siblings would send Mom cards and gifts from themselves and their children. She was always anxious to show off the pictures of her grandkids, along with their thoughtful and carefully chosen gifts.

One memory that always stands out in my mind is of being in the car on a trip to the mall. I noticed that Mom was breathing heavily. She had been a smoker for many years. I nonchalantly commented that she really should quit smoking. She agreed that she really should. End of subject.

Several weeks later, she called to talk, as she often did. At the beginning of the conversation, she announced she had done it—she had quit smoking. When I asked how she did that, she said she just decided to quit. I said I was happy for her and asked if she had a hard time. She answered, "No, not too bad." I asked if she had prayed about it. She said yes, she did. She said she had prayed before to ask God for help, but this time it was different. When I questioned that comment, she said she realized that God would help her, but he wasn't going to do it for her. She put her faith and trust in him. That was Mom, inspirational and strong-willed. She never ceased to amaze me. Our relationship sometimes involved disagreements and frustrations. We had butted heads on more than one occasion. Regardless of that, the mother-daughter bond always remained intact.

Even though Mom stopped smoking, the damage to her lungs was irreversible. She was diagnosed with the early stages of emphysema. She started out with an inhaler, and within a year, her condition worsened, and she needed portable oxygen. She still maintained her pleasant disposition. She was determined to live life as normally as possible. After a while, it became increasingly difficult for her to get out and enjoy doing the things she loved the most. She never complained or indulged in self-pity. I admired her inner strength and perseverance. She continued to be an inspiration to me.

On a Sunday in November 1993, I received a shocking phone call. My oldest brother, who lived near Seattle, had passed away unexpectedly of a heart attack. He was only sixty-two years old. He had always made it a priority to call Mom every Sunday. After the shock of that phone call had begun to sink in, I realized Mom wouldn't be receiving the call she always looked forward to. I would have to find a way to give Mom this heartbreaking news. It was one of the most difficult things I have ever had to do.

I was still married to my first husband at the time, and I was grateful I could lean on him for support. The pain of losing a child is unimaginable to me. When we got in the car to go to Mom's house, I prayed silently: *Please, God, help me to find the words, and please help me to be strong.* When I walked into the house, Mom was sitting in her favorite chair. She looked pale, and I could see that she wasn't feeling well. I got on my knees and held both of her hands. When I told her the bad news, she just looked into my eyes, and her face showed no emotion. I knew she was in shock. I wanted to bring her to our home, but she said she would be okay. We weren't comfortable with leaving her, but she was persistent that she would be all right. We wanted to respect her wishes. Perhaps she needed some time alone to let it sink in.

I cried all the way home. I couldn't believe my big brother was gone. I felt like I was in a waking nightmare. We called to remind Mom we were close by if she needed us. It was among the worst days of our lives.

CHAPTER 15

We were unable to get to Seattle for my brother's funeral. The day after I told Mom the bad news, I drove over to her house to check on her. She still looked pale, and she had developed a cough. I told her I felt she needed to be checked out at the hospital. She looked at me with the trusting eyes of a child and asked if I really thought she should go. I answered, "Yes, Mom, I really think you should." Once again, life had come full circle.

Upon our arrival by ambulance to the hospital, Mom was placed in the intensive care unit. When her condition was stabilized, she was still wide awake. She seemed calm and comfortable as she folded her hands in prayer. I was curious as to exactly what she was praying for. She shook her head to indicate she wasn't praying. She was very weak, and she whispered, "You pray." I honestly don't remember that prayer or what I prayed for. I do know, though, that the Spirit of God was with us. She smiled at me, and then she got some much-needed sleep.

Mom remained in the ICU for fifty-three days, which is rare in the world today. She wanted to be kept alive if she could still communicate with her family. My siblings and other family members came, and if they couldn't be there, they called frequently to see how she was doing. It was difficult for them as well, since they all lived in distant cities.

Mom's oxygen had reached dangerous levels, and it became increasingly more difficult for her to breathe. It was necessary to insert a trach tube in her throat. Her means of communication were now very limited. We either read her lips or she attempted to write things down with her weak and shaky hands. She still could make me laugh. When she was trying to say something and I couldn't understand, she would make a funny face or roll her eyes. Mom's bed was directly in front of the nurses' station, and even the nurses commented on her composure and serenity. The Spirit of the Lord was with her, and he was in both of our hearts; there was no doubt in my mind.

I was still working during Mom's final days. I walked into her room one day, and she had a cast of gray to her complexion. I also noticed the window was wide open. I immediately went to the nurses' station and expressed my concern that she didn't look well, asking why her window was open in February. She could develop pneumonia. The nurse very kindly explained to me that she had asked to have the window open, and they felt it best to honor her wishes.

I sat by Mom's bed and prayed. I said, "Please, God, I can't bear to see her take her last breath." Suddenly, her eyes opened wide, and she was trying to tell me something. I was finally able to understand. She was requesting some McDonald's French fries and a milkshake. After getting an okay from her nurse, I couldn't get to McDonald's quickly enough. I was so sure that she was going to die that day, but God answered my prayer. I know that God hears every prayer, but I also knew it was his will be done, not mine. I began to pray for the strength that only comes from him, the peace that surpasses all human understanding.

A couple days later, I got a call at work telling me that the trach tube was beginning to cause pain in her larynx; to eliminate the pain, they decided to take her in for a short surgery to remove it. A short while later, I received another call from the hospital that I should get there as soon as possible. I arrived at the hospital to find out that Mom had never awakened from the surgery. She died like she lived, with faith and courage. I believe God spared me from my worst fear. She died peacefully in her sleep, and I didn't have to watch her take her last breath. What an awesome God! A friend reminded me of this well-known saying: Death comes with a pain that only God can heal. But it also comes with memories that no one can steal.

One of the most difficult things we encounter is the death of a loved one. I am sure many of you will agree, death comes with a sting that can consume us with sadness. I believe Christ knew how hard death would be for us. In Matthew 14:13 -9 (NIV), he leaves us a message of hope and love: "In my father's house, there are many mansions, if it were not true, I would have told you so. I go to prepare a place for you. And if I go and prepare a place for you I will come again and receive you to myself; that where I am you will be also."

CHAPTER 16

We live in an ever-changing and very troubled world. We continue to pass judgment on one another based on our religious beliefs. We all come from different ethnic cultures, and our lifestyles may differ from one another. It is the lack of love, compassion, and understanding for others that often divides us. In the world, we are constantly exposed to evil. There is no evil that can approach us that cannot be defeated by faith, hope, and love. Every time we listen to the news, we are reminded of the evil that exists among us. Terrorism continues to plague the world, intimidation followed by an act of violence. There was a time when I viewed the source of terror as horrific acts of violence, coming from foreign countries or large groups of people. When I gave it more thought, I realized that terror comes to all of us in different forms. I see the terror of domestic violence, mass murders, bullying, violent protests, child exploitation; the list is endless. I don't believe there is any such thing as the worst of all evils. I can't sugarcoat evil any more than I can sugarcoat good.

God speaks to us about good and evil in Luke 6:45 (NIV): "A good man brings good things out of the love stored up in his heart, and an evil man brings evil things out of the evil up stored in his heart. For the mouth speaks what the heart is full of." If I read and listen closely to his messages to us in the Bible and store up plenty of love in my heart, I can find peace and live without fear. We are all created in the image of our loving Creator. God didn't make me or you different from one another. It is in our human perception of one another that has caused our minds to create our own image of each other—an image that makes us appear to be different. It separates us from one another because sometimes we fail to put forth the good that starts within ourselves, and thus, we cause ourselves to become blind to the good in others.

We are all sinners, and as I grow in faith, I become increasingly more aware of my never-ending need for God's love and mercy. In my relationship with God, he gives me the freedom of will. I can choose to do good in the world and try to follow in his footsteps or I can choose to hold on to resentment or anger. When I make wrong choices and fall into sin, I separate myself from God and become lost in the destruction of self. As I continue my faith journey, my sins begin to lessen, and my love for God becomes greater.

God never said that life would be easy or would come without fear or worry. He has given us the gift of his Spirit that will never leave us. If we explore his loving words in Scripture, through our love and hope in him, we can overcome our fears by taking that leap of faith, placing our trust in him. He created us out of pure love, and good will conquer evil if we all come together for one common cause: to worship him as our Lord and our salvation and follow in his footsteps. Only then can we reflect his goodness. We ourselves can't even scratch the surface to destroy the evil of Satan that is working overtime to destroy souls. God has left us instructions on how to defeat Satan. He refers to this as "body armor" in the book of Ephesians. God knew that our sins would create the chaos and unrest in the world, yet he lovingly told us exactly how to prepare ourselves for battle. There is no greater or more perfect love than his love for mankind.

His promises will come true, and with his help and divine intervention, we can all find happiness in life. The best gift he graced us with is love. Love is the bulletproof vest that sustains us and brings peace to our hearts and souls. We can't always protect ourselves from the physical terror that can lie in wait for us. If we continue to walk in faith, God protects us. A Bible verse that reminds us of this can be found in Jeremiah 29:11: "For I know the thoughts I think towards you, says the Lord, thoughts of peace and not of evil, to give you a future and a hope."

CHAPTER 17

I hope that someday I will see the face of my Creator. No matter what good deeds I do on earth, I know that they are not a ticket to heaven. I must continue to be grateful for his saving grace and use this beautiful gift to remain close to him and continue to follow his ways and surrender to mine. As a human being, my actions do not always emulate God's kindred spirit and infinite goodness. I fall short at times. When I ask for God's forgiveness and don't repeat my sins and fall prey to my defects of character, I have the inner peace of knowing I am forgiven. First, I must seek God's forgiveness before I can ask for the forgiveness of others. It is in forgiveness that we are set free. When we are hurt by the actions or words of others, forgiveness isn't always easy.

About eleven years ago, someone I loved dearly was physically abused. I went to the pastor at a church I attended and asked, "How can I forgive this person?" He said it wasn't going to be easy. It was okay to hate what he did, but I must try not to hate him. The pastor suggested I pray for the abuser. In all honesty, I did not want to pray for him. I wanted someone to inflict the same pain on him that he brought upon a defenseless four-year-old child. I wrestled with that, and as time passed, I finally began the healing process. I had to cling to the fact that she was alive and suffered no physical repercussions as a result of his actions. As far as the emotional effect this had on this precious child, she had received intensive counseling, as did I and others who were affected by this act of violence. I realized, within the healing process, that this man's actions were a direct result of abuse of a mind-altering substance. I was finally able to forgive him by praying that he recovered from his addiction and would never repeat his actions. Today, this beautiful young lady is a happy and remarkably caring and loving person. We return her love with gratitude beyond measure.

When I call upon our Lord for his wisdom and guidance, the hole that was once in my soul is now filled with love and peace. It is no longer filled with doubt and confusion. The void of emptiness is filled with hope. I can never be grateful enough for God's healing of my once-troubled soul. I continue to pray for his intercession in my life. My outlook on life has changed, and I am no longer lost in the darkness of despair. Many things in life can take away our happiness, but I find comfort in knowing it is only temporary. Behind every cloud of darkness lies a rainbow. Being able to see the rainbow among the clouds is a blessing. So many blessings that I was once unable to see are now clear and continue to fill my heart with gratitude.

Life is short, and I have learned, through times of grief, that life is for the living. Being able to move on and appreciate the beautiful moments life brings is another reminder of God's grace. If I continue to live in the moment and cherish the happiness, I will be able to live a life without regret. Awareness of my countless blessings keeps me centered and focused on the joy that comes with faith. If I rush through life, I deprive myself of the beauty and the splendor that began in the loving hands of my Creator. God's gifts to his creation were shaped in the perfection of his hands with his abounding love.

Our all-knowing God continues to place people in my life who inspire and encourage me. If they see that I am drifting off the path, they lovingly suggest that I readjust my sails and take a pathway that will restore me back to serenity. You see, the Spirit of God lies within all of us. We sometimes long to see him, so he makes himself visible to us in his Spirit that resides in the hearts of others. God keeps all his promises to protect us and will never leave us. In Joshua 1:5 (NJKV), he tells us, "No man shall be able to stand before you all the days of your life, as I was with Moses, so I will be with you. I will not leave you nor forsake you."

CHAPTER 18

As I continue my faith journey, God has blessed me with many amazing gifts. My dark days of the past are now in the hands of my Lord and Savior. At times, I try to control life situations, and if I don't remember the importance of placing my trust in God, I create my own struggles. No matter what life throws my way, I know without God's grace I wouldn't be able to fulfill his purpose for me. We are all on a journey in life and in different stages of our journey. There are many ways we can discover the purpose of our existence. As we grow in faith, our direction often changes.

One of the most important truths I try to keep in mind is Christ's words in Romans 12:10 (NKJV): "Be kindly affectionate to one another with brotherly love, in honor giving preference to one another." They are many ways we can show our love for one another. I believe we can find our purpose in life within God's Word. We live in a world of starvation, not only in a literal sense but in a spiritual sense. Our world lacks love. If we love, honor, and cherish our Creator, then we can love, honor, and cherish one another.

I don't believe God created us to be unhappy. Look at the world; he created so much beauty to bring us happiness—a newborn baby, the stars, the beautiful sunsets, to name just a few. The most beautiful gift Christ gave us was himself. He showed us how to live with kindness and compassion, and then, when he sacrificed his life for us, he showed us how to die with love and courage.

There are times when I still question things. I don't know why little babies or young people leave this earth so soon. Any negative thoughts are always defeated by thoughts of hope and trust in

God's plan. When I share my thoughts with other believers, if I am troubled, they throw me a lifejacket. They gently remind me that I must remain faithful and that faith requires action. God has placed me among a large group of people, and the prayer circle that begun with those little children has continued. We pray for one another, for ourselves, and for anyone who expresses a need for prayer. It doesn't matter what church they attend or even if they attend a church. If they believe that praying will bring them God's comfort, then it is an honor and responsibility to pray for them. I find solace when I seek out God's words in the Bible and connect them to prayer. Not only did Christ show us his perfect love, but he left all of us those love messages to comfort and reassure us. He has also given us warnings of the consequences of our actions that are not pleasing to him. As our loving Father, he has commanded us to love one another as he has loved us. First Corinthians 13:13 says, "And now abide faith, hope, and love, these three; but the greatest of these is love."

If you don't believe in the existence of God, then who am I to judge? Faith does not make me better than you. It is only through grace and faith that we can all receive the gifts of God. So keep in mind that if I, who was once a nonbeliever, can be awakened to the spirit within myself, then so can anyone else who is living in doubt. I think perhaps it is people like me and others who are the weeds in God's garden. Not the weeds he wants to destroy; we are the weeds he transforms from a dormant little seed, and he brings us back to life.

If you are one of the weeds in God's garden, I hope you will find peace and happiness and the faith to believe that there is a power within yourself, a power much greater than you. That power is love, for God *is* love! You also can be restored back to life. May the love From the Heart of the Spirit be with you today and in all the days to come.

If you are agnostic like I once was and don't believe in the power of prayer, then I hope you will keep this book. God works in ways that are wondrous and strange, yet there is nothing in life that God cannot change if you open your heart and mind and never give up hope. Remember that God loves all of us, whether we believe it or not!

I don't know if it is God's will for this book to be published, but I know it was important for me to write it. I always want to keep it fresh in my mind that through God's patience and grace, he has helped me move from darkness to light, from despair to healing, and from doubt to faith.

PRAYERS FROM THE HEART OF THE SPIRIT

Heavenly Father, we come before you today with love and gratitude in our hearts. Thank you for your unconditional love. Our hope is in you. Sometimes life can bring on anger and frustrations. We get frustrated with our families, our jobs, people we encounter during our day. We ask for your guidance, Lord. help us to be an image of you and a reflection of your love. When we are tempted to lash out at others, saying unkind words, we ask that you soften our hearts. help us to have the discipline we need to be respectful to one another. When temptation arises, we have hope that we will call upon your name before we act without praying for your help. Bless us, Lord, so that we can be a blessing to others. In Jesus's name, we pray. Amen.

Proverbs 10:22: "The blessing of the Lord makes one rich and He adds no sorrow to it."

Our Lord, thank you for another day. Hope in you is such a blessing. So many people need our prayers. May we never forget that we need to pray for ourselves first. We can't ask for prayers for others if we aren't talking to you first. Help us, Lord, to come to you always when our hearts are troubled. Through our prayers to you, our prayers for others will be said through your Spirit of guidance. Thank you, God, not only for the hope we have in you, but for your guidance. In Jesus's name, we pray. Amen.

Psalm 31:24: "Be of good courage and he shall strengthen your heart, All you who hope in the Lord.

Dear Father, you are truly an amazing God! I love when you speak to us through others. You place people in our lives to confide in when we are struggling with something. When we are ungrateful, please help us to open our eyes to our blessings so that we can see your goodness. You, our heavenly Father, are love. And you speak softly to us through others when we need comfort and good directions. Through your spirit of love, you bring us inner peace. May our hearts be open and our minds willing to listen when you speak to us. To you be the glory, now and forever, amen.

Proverbs 1:5: Let the wise listen and add to their learning, and let the discerning get guidance.

Sometimes, Lord, we can be very selfish and self-centered. We don't always like to face that fact. Often we put ourselves first. We want to be first in the shopping lines or any lines where we must be patient and wait our turn. We think that what we are trying to accomplish is more important than what those around us are trying to do. We need your help, Lord, because we are also selfish with our time. We would rather do what we enjoy most than spend some time in a nursing home or visiting the sick or the shut-ins. These actions or lack of actions are not a reflection of you, our heavenly Father. Make us mindful, Lord, to live as you have lived and to do as you have done. We seek your forgiveness, and we ask your help so that we can all become less selfish and more giving. We call out to you in Jesus's name, amen.

Philippians 2:3: "Let nothing be done through selfish ambition or conceit, but in lowliness of mind let each esteem others better than himself."

Our Lord, sometimes we must make difficult decisions in life. Some may concern our families, our health, our jobs, and even political decisions. May we honor and praise your name by looking to you for the answers. We can't make any decisions that give us peace of mind if we don't seek your wisdom through prayer and patience. You know all things, our heavenly Father, and our futures are in your hands. You want us, Father God, to change our hearts so that we can be one with you who have created us. Help us, Lord, to accept you and your will and not concede to our will. We need your help, Lord, for you are our pathway to eternal life. In Jesus's precious name we pray. Amen.

Matthew 6:33: "But seek first the Kingdom of God and his righteousness, and all these things will be added to you."

Our Father, we pray for all the little children in the world, your precious little ones who are barely staying alive without food and water. For those who have become physically ill, abused, ignored, bullied, and have gone without parental love and supervision. It is heartbreaking, Lord, that through no fault of their own, they are exposed to such suffering. We ask you, Father, to watch over them. Please place people in their lives to protect and guide them. There are those little ones who have not had the opportunity to know you. They are surrounded by the violence and tragedy of war. It is so sad, Lord, but you are a powerful God who can do all things! Please bless them with your unconditional love. Surround your little children with your angels to watch over them and protect them from harm. You so loved the little children when you became man and walked the earth. Your faithfulness helps us to feel hopeful, Lord, that you will take away their suffering. In your holy name, we pray, Amen.

Genesis 50:21: "Now therefore, do not be afraid; I will provide for you and your little ones. And he comforted them and spoke kindly to them."

Nina Austin

Heavenly Father, you have commanded us to love one another. Sometimes that can be a challenge, especially when we strongly disagree with someone, or maybe we are holding resentment toward someone or them toward ourselves. You have shown us the power of forgiveness. So help us today, Lord, to remember your command to love one another as you have loved us. We come before you with humility, Lord. Help us to overcome our animosity toward one another. Help us to help ourselves take away any anger, resentment, or anything that causes us to sin against you. We want to choose your way and not ours, holy Father. Please help us to let go of any unkind feelings toward others that are separating us from you. We pray with reverence to your holy name. Amen.

Psalm 18:21: "For I have kept the ways of the Lord; I am not guilty of turning from my God."

Our great God, we thank you for your love and forgiveness. Sometimes we don't think before we speak. You came to earth to teach us how to live in peace and harmony with one another. Then you loved us enough to die for our sins! The ultimate sacrifice, the greatest, most perfect love. Help us when we make bad decisions that result in our sins. Our prayer today is that we will always seek your forgiveness and show that we are sorry by repenting for our sins. You are a merciful and loving God. May we be slow to anger and quick to forgive. Guide our hearts, Lord, so that we do not hesitate to seek your forgiveness when we sin. Also, when we are unkind to one another and we fail to forgive, then we ask for your mercy. Change our hearts, Lord, so that we live a life that is pleasing to you. You are the sole purpose for our existence, so we hope we will always put you first among all else. Our desire is to be the people you have created us to be. We pray with humility in memory of your life and Your death on Calvary and your promise of eternal life. Thank you, Father God, for your unconditional love. Help us to be faithful to you in all that we do. In your holy name, we offer this prayer to you. Amen.

Psalm 86:15: "But you, Lord are a compassionate and gracious God; slow to anger and abounding in love and faithfulness."

Nina Austin

Our Lord, when we prepare to celebrate the Christian holidays, we ask that we be a good example for all the world to see. When we celebrate Thanksgiving, may we always remember to come before you with a thankful heart—not just on Thanksgiving Day but every day. During the season of Lent, we place ourselves in your hands as we remember your crucifixion and death for our sins on the cross at Calvary. When we celebrate Easter, we remember your glorious resurrection from the dead. We not only recall your rising from the dead, we remember all the signs of the spring and new birth. The flowers begin to come back to life, just as you did! During Advent, we prepare to celebrate your birth. May we always remember the reason for each season. At Christmastime, we want to remember that you are always the reason for the season. We celebrate your birth as the Christ child, the beginning of your life on earth! Help us to be a living example of your life and the meaning of each special Christian celebration. Help us not to get lost in the materialistic things and celebrate the true meaning of each holy occasion. May we live and celebrate in a way that others will recognize the sacred meaning of each season. May we always bring honor and glory to your name. In memory of your gifts to the world we offer this prayer to you. Amen.

1 Chronicles 16:29: "Give to the Lord the Glory due his name; bring an offering and come before him, oh worship the Lord in the beauty of his holiness."

Our Lord, when you created the heavens and the earth, it was beautiful. You created all of us so we can enjoy the splendor of all your creation. So much beauty can be found, if we just slow down and take the time to enjoy it. The four seasons, the vivacious colors of the flowers in spring; the warmth of the sun with its breathtaking sunsets in the summer; the vivid colors of the trees as they change colors in the fall; and in the winter, the pure whiteness of the snow. You have given us the gift of awareness. Help us, Lord, to be grateful for our blessings and to gently remind others of your beautiful creation, made from your love for all the people in your universe to enjoy. You have given us these gifts to bring adoration and praise to your name. Without you as our Savior, our confidant and protector, we would fall into the darkness of despair and the sorrow of living without you. Please guide our hearts so that our minds are open. We know, Lord, without you in our lives, our gift of life would be meaningless. Thank you for placing us in the beauty of your creation, Lord, and may the light of hope shine bright within us Almighty Father. In Jesus's name, we offer this prayer to you. Amen.

Psalm 139:12: "Even the darkness will not be dark **to** you; the night will shine like the day, for darkness is as light to you."

Lord, our need for you is crucial, and we honor your holy name and give you glory for the daily reminders that you bring to our attention. You have blessed us with the wisdom and knowledge to recognize this never-ending need for you in our lives. Let no evil separate us from you as we walk with you through this life you have created just for us. Thank you, Lord Jesus. Your gift of life replenishes our souls and awakens us to your infinite love and salvation. You are the light that cannot be overcome by darkness. With gratitude, we thank you, Father God, for placing us in the safety of your light. Amen.

John 8:12: "When Jesus spoke again to the people he said, "I am the light of the world. Whoever follows me will never walk in darkness, but will have the light of life."

Nina Austin

Abba God, we give you thanks for your wondrous ways. We praise and thank you for loving us regardless of our many shortcomings. Today we ask that you teach us—not only to pray, but equally as important to be good listeners. We ask for clarity of our minds, to find that quiet place where you can work within us and through us as we follow in your footsteps. When you left your disciples to pray to your Father, he spoke to your heart to give you the courage to carry on. We seek your help to be more like you who have created us in your perfect image. In memory of your life and death we pray. Amen.

Mark 1:35 (Jesus prays in solitude) "Very early in the morning while it was still dark Jesus got up and went to a solitary place where He could pray."

Almighty loving Father, your loving ways are so comforting. You have kept your promise never to abandon us. Thank you for the times we have been open to receive your peace. Your nearness blesses us with your peace, both in the good days in life and the difficult days. We never need to feel alone, for you are right here with us. We continue to pray with perseverance to carry us through the storms of life. Thank you, God, for your peace, encouragement, and guidance. Most of all your love! Amen.

Philippians 4:7: "And the peace of God, which transcends all understanding, will guard your hearts and your minds in Christ Jesus."

Lord, we give you thanks and praise for another day, another chance to make a difference in the world. We pray for those who have yet to accept your saving grace. May we set a good example for them, and may our actions speak louder than any words we say. Bless them, Lord. May we be always humble and never judge them, but be willing to share our gift of faith with them. If they are living in spiritual darkness, then we pray, dear Lord, that you lift them out of the darkness and hold them in the palm of your hand. It is with great hope in you that they will find you, and it is with humility that we ask you to save them. We offer this prayer to you, Almighty God, with hope and praise. Amen.

Ephesians 2:8: "For it is by grace you have been saved through faith—and it is not of yourselves. It is the gift of God.

Father God, you are the King of kings. We bow down before you to worship you with purity of heart. It is through your mercy that we can come before you with hope. Let no other try to distract us or no evil to approach us. We thank you today, Lord, for casting away all the evil that desires to separate us from you. You crush Satan beneath your feet. We humble ourselves before you as we ask for forgiveness for our sins. As you sit on your heavenly throne, we offer you our gifts of gratitude and love, now and forever. Amen.

Psalm 30:12: "To the end that my glory may sing praise to you and not be silent. O Lord, my God, I will give thanks to you forever."

Nina Austin

Our Lord, we have heard it said that "time is of the essence." Help us, Father, to spend time alone with you. We don't always make time to come to you in our daily routine. Your powerful ways speak to us through the gentleness of your spirit, dear Lord. Open our ears to hear your Word and to use your words in Scripture to help others who are feeling lost, alone, and discouraged. May we spend our quiet time alone with you to grow in our love for you. May we always use the time you have given us to continue to feel and embrace your blessings with a grateful heart. Help us, Lord, to spend time with you every day. In the name of Jesus, our rock and our salvation, we pray. Amen.

Ecclesiastes 3–4 (A time for everything): "There is a time for everything and a season for every activity under the heavens; a time to be born and a time to die, a time to plant and a time to uproot, a time to kill and a time to heal. A time to tear down and a time to rebuild, a time to weep and a time to laugh, a time to mourn and a time to dance."

Dear Lord, thank you for your words to us in Scripture. You have left us with your great words of your power and your love. Your words give us strength in times of weakness, hope to replace doubts, and grace to believe. We give you praise, our all-powerful God! We bring honor and glory to your name, today and every day. Your words to us in Scripture keep us on the path of righteousness, peace, and love for you. This helps us to spread your peace to those around us, to all our brothers and sisters in your creation. In the name of Christ Jesus, we pray. Amen.

2 Thessalonians 2:14: "He called you to this through our gospel, that you may share in the glory of our Lord Jesus Christ."

Our Creator, sometimes life can throw some difficult and painful situations our way. People lose their loved ones due to natural disasters, illness, accidents, and the evil of hate crimes. When these things happen, you never leave us. You offer compassion and peace to those who are suffering these horrific losses. We see your face through the faces of other believers. No matter what happens in life, you have assured us that you remain the same. You speak to us about this in Hebrews 13:8: "Jesus Christ is the same yesterday, today, and forever." That, Lord, refreshes and renews our awareness of your ability to do all things! You are the King of kings and the salvation of mankind. We give you thanks today and every day. You want us to be happy in life. Thank you, Lord Jesus, for comforting us when those difficult times come our way. In your most holy name we pray. Amen.

Romans 15:33: "The peace of God be with you all. Amen."

Our God, on this day, we come to you with thanksgiving. Without your presence in our lives, we would be lost and alone. The void we would feel would be unbearable and leave us feeling empty and lost inside. Your constant reminders of your love are like the fuel that lights the fire of your Holy Spirit that dwells within us. Your salvation, perfect peace, patience, and guidance are the beautiful gifts that we will never have to live without. You are the potter, and we are the clay. You mold us into the people that you have created us to be. You bring us peace that only you, Lord Jesus, can bring. We worship you above all things. Thank you for your ultimate gift, your act of perfect love on Calvary. In honor of you who are the power that holds us and unites us together with one another, we worship you above all things. In memory of your sacrifice of love, we offer up this prayer to you in Jesus's name. Amen.

Chronicles 1 16:34: "Give thanks to the Lord for he is good; his love endures forever."

Today, our Lord, we come before you to lift those who are poor in spirit. Maybe they have lost a loved one and are struggling to try to understand why. Or perhaps someone has been praying for something, and they feel that you have not answered their prayers. Many people find, in the blink of an eye, their lives can change dramatically. They may suffer in an accident and find themselves crippled. The devastation of divorce or an unfaithful spouse may crush their spirits. Our hearts can be troubled sometimes, and we may not understand why things happen as they do. When these things occur, we come to you to pray that our spirits and the spirts of others become renewed. In Jesus's name, we pray. Amen.

Matthew 5:3: "Blessed be the poor in spirit for theirs is the kingdom of heaven."

Dear God, you are such a faithful God! You have spoken to us about the importance of praying without ceasing. When we do that, we can see your powerful responses to our prayers. When we sin, we can feel your faithfulness to forgive, if we turn away from our sins and pray for strength when temptation arises. You are always faithful in your love for us. When we remain faithful to you, we can feel your loving presence. Help us today, Lord, to always return your faithfulness and keep your commandments. For it is you, God, who is worthy of all our love and obedience. In the name of Christ Jesus, we pray. Amen.

Deuteronomy 7:9: "Know therefore the Lord your God is God; he is the faithful God keeping his covenant of love to thousands of generations to those who love him and keep his commandments."

Our great God, thank you for waking us up today. How easy it could be to take our lives for granted. By coming to you in prayer, we humble ourselves and we remember that it is you, God, who are in control of our lives. We sometimes like to be in control, thinking we know all the answers. But it always takes us back to you, where we need to be! Thank you for making us aware of that today, Lord. No matter what we do in life, it is you who holds all power and control. We may have a position in our jobs where we may be in control of many people; in some cases, that can bring out our ego. We continue to humbly place ourselves before you and acknowledge that it is you who rules our lives. Forgive us, Lord, for the times when our ego gets in the way and we think we are so important. Without you in our lives, we are nothing. To you we surrender our ego and we are grateful that you hold us in the palm of your hand and you grant us your peace. We pray with gratitude to you. We ask that you help destroy our ego or anything that could cause us to separate ourselves from you. In Jesus's name, we pray. Amen.

James 4:10: "Humble yourselves before the Lord and he will lift you up."

Thank you, heavenly Father, for creating us and giving us the gift of life. Thank you also for another day and another chance to live our lives in a way that is pleasing to you and will make this world a better place. If we love one another and help each other, then we can, through you, make a difference in this life you have given us and the world around us. You truly are an amazing God! May we always find a way to express our love for you first, and then we have hope that our love will blossom out to others. Sometimes just a smile or an act of kindness can change someone's heart. With you by our side, life becomes meaningful as we fall to our knees to honor you above all else. If we stay close to you, there is nothing you cannot or will not do to help us for the good of your name. Thank you, God, for this beautiful gift of life! Amen.

Luke 10:27: "Love the Lord your God with all your heart and with all your soul and with all your strength and with all your minds; and love your neighbor as yourself."

Our heavenly Father, you know all things. You know what is on our minds and what is in our hearts. You know when we are truly sorry and when we are not. We can never keep anything from you. You are an all-knowing, all-loving God. Do we know you though, God? Thank you for giving us the Bible so that we can learn about you and know you! We can know you intimately when we spend quiet time alone with you. We can have conversations with you that are pleasing and meaningful to you. Thank you, Father. Today we are grateful for the knowledge that if we follow your ways and not our ways, we will not only know you, but we will grow in our love for you. We have hope that someday we will see your face! Glory, honor, praise, and love to you, our heavenly Father, now and forever. Amen.

Romans 8:28: "And we know in all things God works for those who love him, who have been called according to his purpose."

Abba, you are truth and love. Your love knows no boundaries. It is so intense that it is incomprehensible to our human ability to understand. You have created within us the capacity to love. Our love can never be compared to your perfect love! Without your great love, we would be lost without hope of eternal life. Thank you, Abba, for your unconditional love. As a human father or mother, we think our love for our children could not be greater. It is a pure and good love, but nothing exceeds your bountiful love for all your creation. Thank you, Lord, for the priceless gift of your love for us. In memory of your Son, Jesus Christ, we pray. Amen.

John 15:13: "Greater love has no one than this, than to lay down one's life for his friends."

Our merciful Father, as we begin another new day, we place our cares in your hands. No matter what awaits us on this day, we invite you to walk with us in your loving and gentle spirit. Keep us from any unnecessary worry or stress that we may bring upon ourselves. You have told us in the Scriptures about the uselessness of worry. In Matthew 6:27, you told us, "Can any one of you by worrying add a single hour to your life?" Thank you God, for reminding us that we should cast all our worries upon you and place our trust in you, that whenever our hearts our troubled you are in control of every situation that occurs in our lives. Many times, we worry about our children, our financial state, our health, the health of our loved ones, the world around us; the list is endless, Lord. So, on this day, we will trust you that all will be well and exactly as your perfect plan for us has been made. With love and trust in your power and might we pray. Amen.

Proverbs 3:6–7 "In all your ways submit to him, and he will make your paths straight." Do not be wise in your own eyes: fear the Lord and shun evil."

Nina Austin

Today Lord, we thank you for the gift of faith; for the ability to be open to receive your grace and to believe in the power of our prayers to you. Thank you, Lord, for these amazing blessings! Thank you for opening our eyes to the needs of others. If we are not seeing past ourselves and realizing the needs of others, then we ask for your guidance and help. We all have problems, Lord, but if we look around us, we can always find someone whose problems are greater than our own. You are our refuge and our strength in both challenging times and in times of joy! You calm our fears when we talk to you about them, and it is your strength and your courage that gives us hope. No matter what life brings our way today, we humble ourselves before you and we ask for your forgiveness and your mercy for the times when we have put you aside and allowed other things to be first in our lives. May we always place you first before all things, Father God, and may we be a shining example of Christian love. Our hope is that we will always trust in your plans for us. You are the way, the truth, and the light. In Jesus's name, we pray. Amen.

John 8:12: "When Jesus spoke to the people, he said," I am the light of the world. Whoever follows me will not walk in darkness, but will have the light of life.

Our Lord, in this troubled world, you are our hope. Your love messages you left us in the Scriptures remind us that you loved us enough to die for us. You are a loving, forgiving God. When we follow your commandments, you do not want us to be fearful or anxious. You are a just and powerful God. You strengthen us, protect us, and will never leave us. Lord, if ever we let go of you and start to drift away from you, then please keep hold of our hearts and minds so we won't stray away from you. In Jesus's name, we praise you now and through all eternity. Amen.

Isaiah 41:10: "So do not fear, for I am with you; do not be dismayed, for I am your God. I will strengthen you and help you; I will uphold you with my righteous right hand."

Today, our merciful God, we remind ourselves again the importance of putting aside our private time to "Be still and know that you are God." You have asked us to pray with perseverance. We also ask for your help to remember that it is equally important to meditate and listen quietly for your answers. Often, we see and hear you through the voices of others, but only if we listen. We love you, Lord Jesus, and we don't want one-sided conversations with you with ourselves doing all the talking. Thank you, Lord, for keeping your promise to never leave us! We pray in Jesus's name. Amen.

Psalm 46:10: "Be still and know that I am God; I will be exulted among the nations; I will be exulted in the earth."

Dear God, often we find ourselves quick to anger. Sometimes anger is a good thing, if we are angry about the injustice in the world and we try to do our part to change it. Many times, though, our anger is not justifiable. We become angry at family members, friends, and even complete strangers. We lose patience and say words that are hurtful and damaging to others. Our actions are not always Christ-like and pleasing to you. Once those words leave our mouths, we can't take them back. Help us, Lord, to think and pray before we speak. We ask for your forgiveness for the times we have sinned against you. We also plead with you to bless us so that we can ask forgiveness from those we have hurt and to show our remorse by not repeating our words or actions. In your most precious name, we thank you for your grace to forgive us, and we pray for your grace to seek the forgiveness of others. Amen.

1 John 1:9: "If we confess our sins, he is faithful and just and will forgive us our sins and to purify us from all unrighteousness."

Nina Austin

Acceptance isn't always easy, Lord. People pull out in front of us in traffic, and we observe them talking on their cell phones, paying no attention to what they're doing. Other people are just plain rude, and it is sometimes hard to accept their behavior. Then we have those who are running for the presidency, and they say things that make us question their integrity. But then, Lord, we remember the foolish things we have said and done. You accept us, Lord, and when we keep that in mind, it makes us think of not only acceptance but humility. Who are we to judge others when we are all sinners? We should, with your help, make hard decisions regarding those who are seeking a position of authority. This calls to our attention the serenity prayer. Lord, Grant us the serenity to accept the things we cannot change, the courage to change the things we can, and the wisdom to know the difference. Through this prayer to you, we will find acceptance and peace. On this day, Lord, and all the days to follow, we will need your help to remind us that acceptance is the pathway to peace. Thank you for being so patient with us, Lord. We pray with humility and love. Amen.

Psalm 6:9: "The Lord has heard my cry for mercy; the lord accepts my prayer."

Dear God, just listening to the news can be a frightening experience—senseless loss of human lives due to murder, suicide, terrible hate crimes, corrupt politicians, drug and alcohol abuse, and racial discrimination. It feels as if we are surrounded by evil and fear. Yet you have told us in Job 11:14, "If you put away the sin, the sin that is in your hands, and allow no evil to dwell in your tent (home/heart) we will lift your head without shame and stand firm and without fear." What comfort and hope your words bring to us! If we continue to stay focused on you and obey your commandments, then we have nothing to fear! What a faithful God we serve! We ask you, sweet Jesus, to open the hearts and minds of those who have yet to find faith in you and don't know of your great love for them. For those who are in the darkness of constant sin, we ask you, our God, to help them and all of us to turn away from any evil ways and find peace and trust through you. In Jesus's holy name we pray. Amen.

Isaiah 26:3: "You will keep in perfect peace those whose minds are steadfast, because they trust in you."

Our holy Father, so many times we come before you in prayer and make our petitions known to you. We express to you our hearts' desires, be it for our loved ones, our friends, or ourselves. We continually ask for your intervention in our lives and the lives of others. How often, though, do we sit in silence and listen, taking time out to reflect on your goodness and to wait for you to speak to our hearts? We forget, our Father, that it is as important for us to listen as it is to pray—to take that special quiet time we can spend alone with you. We long to have an intimate relationship with you that enables us to listen quietly for your loving wisdom and guidance. As we feel your spirit of truth, we can open our hearts to receive your blessings. In Jesus's name, we offer this prayer to you. Amen.

Proverbs 1:5: "Let the wise listen and add to their learning and the discerning get guidance."

Dear Lord, we come before you this day to worship you and thank you for giving us another day to do your will. So many things in life try to distract us from looking toward you for comfort and strength. Maybe it is a busy, frustrating day at work or an unexpected bill, another annoying driver on the road. But Lord, please help us to take time, no matter how short the prayer may be, to acknowledge you, and then we can change our own attitude toward others and we can hopefully change our hearts and set a good example for them, to encourage them, by setting a good example for them. We can always begin our day over, at any given moment if need be, and invite you to walk with us. We aren't worthy of your love, Father God, but you continue to care for us and to welcome us to be one with you through your saving grace. Thank you, Lord Jesus, for your endless love. Amen.

Psalm 70:4 But may all who seek you rejoice and be glad in you: may those who long for your saving help always say, "The Lord is great!"

Gracious God, we are in awe of your almighty power to heal—not only the physical healing but the spiritual and emotional healing you provide to all who cry out to you in our times of need. You are a just and merciful God. Your faithfulness through your words to us shines like a beacon of light. If we struggle to see your truths, you carry us during those times when it seems like an effort to get through the day. We thank you, God, for keeping your promise to never abandon us. You are the holy one! The Alpha and the Omega. We humbly offer this prayer to you with love and adoration. Amen.

Revelation 22:13: "I am the Alpha and the Omega, the First and the Last, the Beginning and the End."

Abba, as we embrace this new day, we thank you and give you praise for our blessings, too numerous to count! May we never take you for granted. Your salvation, forgiveness, love, patience, and guidance are the most important gifts you have blessed us with. There is no earthly gift as precious or as priceless as your gifts to mankind. May our gifts to you be faithfulness in all that we do, and may we share our blessings and gifts with others. You are the King of peace, our Father. Thank you for granting us your grace to know that there is not one prayer to you that goes unheard. Thank you, Father. This brings us serenity and hope of spending all eternity in your presence. May we live this day by bringing honor and glory to your name, not just today but in all the days to follow. In memory of your Son, Jesus, we pray. Amen.

Deuteronomy 16:17: "Each of you must bring a gift in proportion to the way the Lord Your God has blessed you."

Dear God, sometimes doing the right thing takes courage. Deciding to share our faith with others can put us at risk of being ridiculed. When you think about your life, you were constantly been ridiculed. Yet you carried that burden with courage and love. We can be accused of being self-righteous, Bible thumpers, holier than thou, and all kinds of criticism. So we call upon your name for your advice. Help us to always approach others with humility. If we set a good example, sometimes no words are necessary, and we can reflect you by our actions. You have enough love in the heart of your spirit for all your creation! Help us, dear Lord, to remember that we are all on a faith journey, and we are all at different stages of our journey with you. Our prayer today is that all our paths will ultimately lead to you. We pray with humility and hope in you. Amen.

Philippians 2:3: "Do nothing out of selfish ambition or vain conceit, rather, in humility value others above yourself."

Our precious God, we offer this prayer today for all those who have been caught up in the terror of war. We have been reminded that you, Lord Jesus, are the only one who was willing to sacrifice your life to offer salvation to the world. Only you, God, made that ultimate sacrifice through your Son, Christ Jesus. Before you sent the Messiah, there had always been wars. Some were necessary to come to the aid of humanity. Other wars were brought on by greed, the quest for power, or pure evil. We humbly ask that you bless the men and women who have lost their lives or have become physically and emotionally disabled as a result of the horrible trauma and terror of war. Bless them, Lord, and we pray that they find peace through you and your saving grace. Please watch over them and their families and help us all to reach out to them and to do something, no matter how small or how big, to provide for them. In Jesus's most holy name we pray. Amen.

Isaiah 25:8: "He will swallow up death forever. The sovereign Lord will wipe away the tears from all faces; he will remove his people's disgrace from all the earth. The Lord has spoken."

Our loving God, when we celebrate Valentine's Day, the day we set aside to show extra love to those closest to our hearts, we give one another candy, cards, and dinners out. How shall we celebrate you on this day of love and gift giving? We can honor your name and give you thanks and praise. But we should do this every day. So, what can we do differently on this day? We can't really do anything that we shouldn't be doing already. Perhaps today we can reflect again on your love and recognize it as the ultimate love. There is no love greater than yours. May we all remember on Valentine's Day that you are the Father of love. So, as we remember that love began with you, the most beautiful gift of all, we thank you for your perfect love. In memory of Christ Jesus we pray. Amen.

Colossians 3:14: "And over all these virtues put on love which binds them all in perfect unity."

Dearest Lord, the word that comes to mind today is *trust*. Sometimes it is a struggle to trust. Marriages are destroyed because of lack of trust. Friendships are destroyed; we lack trust in government leaders; we don't trust those who have betrayed a confidence; yet you, Lord, are worthy of our complete trust. A huge part of our faith is having trust in you. Thank you for encouraging us, as we have learned about your faithful love that has no end. With trust in you comes the ties that bind us together so that we can live in harmony with one another and most importantly with you. For that, Lord, we are forever grateful. In Christ Jesus's name we pray. Amen.

Isaiah 26:3: "You will keep him in perfect peace whose mind are steadfast, because they trust in you."

Thank you, Lord Jesus, for all the beautiful gifts you have blessed us with. For the sunshine, the stars in the sky, the trees, and the miracle of a newborn baby's life. May we never overlook the joy and happiness that any of your gifts bring to us. For you are worthy, Lord, of all our glorious praise. May we continue to thank you for your wondrous ways. For you are the Messiah, the King of kings, and our salvation. In Jesus's name, we offer this prayer to you. Amen.

1 Chronicles 29:13: "Now, our God, we give you thanks and praise your glorious ways."

Our heavenly Father, we ask that your blessings be upon all of those who are sick and suffering. You hold the power to heal physically, emotionally, and spiritually. We ask that you bless them and take away their pain. Give them your peace, our heavenly Father, and restore them to good health. If this is not your will for them, then we pray for acceptance. Provide for them comfort and trust in you. Take away their distress and send your angels to watch over them. Our hope is in you, Lord. We ask this in Jesus's name. Amen.

Jeremiah 33:6: "Nevertheless I will bring health and healing to it. I will heal my people and let them enjoy abundant peace and security."

Our Father, we thank you for our countless blessings. We rejoice in the season of spring and rebirth. As the flowers begin to bloom, we rejoice in the beauty of your creation. We never walk alone in our journey with you. Your spirit of love and truth is always with us. We pray that it always remains with us, so that together we can become one with you. Thank you, Lord Jesus, for all the beautiful gifts you have given us. Our families and friends you have placed in our lives are gifts to be cherished. As we stay close to you, our sins will become less and our love for you greater. We offer this prayer to you with gratitude in our hearts. You are our God! The purpose of our lives is to be obedient to you, to bow down before you with glory and praise to your holy name. Amen.

1 John 4:8: "For whoever does not know love does not know God. For God is love."

Our Lord, when we desire to accomplish something, when we have come so close to our goals, we encounter roadblocks. This can be very frustrating. You spoke of the emotions you encountered when you became man. You felt anger when you destroyed the evil in the temple. You were scorned, ridiculed, doubted, and finally put to an agonizing death. You never gave in to your emotions. You prayed to your Father, and he strengthened you. Bless us, O Lord, so we don't allow our human emotions to cause us to want to give up. We desire to be more like you and put our emotions in your hands through our prayers to you. So we humbly ask, Father God, that you give us the strength to carry on. We pray today that when life becomes discouraging, or when we are afraid, we will let go of whatever negative emotions we feel and place our trust in you. Amen.

Joshua 1:9: "Have I not commanded you? Be strong and courageous; do not be afraid: for the Lord your God will be with you wherever you go."

Our God, you are the one and only true God, the Father of truth and love. Your love is endless! It knows no boundaries! It is so intense that it is beyond our human understanding. What a great God we serve! You have birthed within us the capability to love. Our love can never be compared to yours. Your love is flawless and perfect. Without your great love for all your children, we would all be lost and alone. Nothing exceeds your bountiful, unconditional love for all your creation. Thank you for the animals you have placed in our lives to care for and love. Thank you, Lord, for the priceless gift of your perfect love. In memory of Christ, our Lord and Savior, we give thanks and praise to your holy name. Amen.

John 1:14" The Word became flesh and made his dwelling among us. We have seen his glory, the glory of the one and only Son, who came from the Father, full of grace and truth."

Nina Austin

Dear God, sometimes we can consume ourselves with worry and fear. We worry about our finances, our families, and success in the workplace. We worry about our health and the health of those we love. Many of the things we waste precious time worrying about never happen. We become so obsessed with worry that we miss out on the things you want to bring to us, peace and joy. Today we ask your help in focusing on the here and now. Help us, Lord, to live in the beautiful moments that you have created for us. Grant us your peace so that we can offer up all our worries to you. You wait patiently until we are ready to trust in you. We need help letting go and letting you, Lord, take away our worries and cares. Our worries continue to mount and sometimes prevent us from trusting you enough to place our worries in your care and leave them there. Thank you, our loving God, for your willingness to bear our burdens for us. We praise you with gratitude, Lord Jesus. Amen.

Psalm 68:19 "Praise be to the Lord, to God our Savior, who daily bears our burdens."

Holy Lord, we are surrounded by genocide across the globe. We are in dire need of your healing. Not only have you used your physical and spiritual power to heal, you have the almighty power to change all that is happening in the world today. Help us not to hate because others believe differently than we do. Help us to see one another with compassion and not animosity or rash judgment. You have told us to love our enemies. That is difficult, Lord. We must stop those whose evil desire is to harm or kill us, but we pray that we will not allow hate to reside in our hearts. We stand firm on the grace and faith that you have blessed us with. Help us, Lord, to remain faithful to your Word and remove hate from our thoughts and actions. In Jesus's name, we place our hope and trust in you. Amen.

Proverbs 3:5-6 "Trust in the Lord with all your heart and do not rely on your own understanding; in all ways submit to him and he shall make your paths straight and narrow."

Lord, as we come before you this day, we examine our hearts and our consciences. We want to be pure in heart, our Father, as we place our prayer petitions before you. We ask that your supreme power be with us and with the world around us. Help us always to stand up for our faith in you, regardless of what others may think of us. Your greatness is worthy of sharing with those around us. Take away any pride or any obstacle that wants to prevent us from being an instrument of your peace. For all that we are that is good, we give you thanks. You are our awesome God, and there is nothing we want to do to prevent ourselves and others from giving you the honor and praise that belongs to you and only you! We offer this prayer to you today, and we thank you for being an awesome God whose love for us is unconditional.

Ephesians 5:20: "Giving thanks always for all things to God the Father in the name of our Lord Jesus Christ."

Our loving God, we offer up many prayers to you. We thank you for the prayers answered. What about those prayers that we sometimes feel are not answered? For instance, when we plead with you to heal a loved one and your will is to call them home. Does that mean that you didn't answer our prayers? I don't believe so, Lord. Acceptance of your will is not always easy. I have heard others say you answer prayers in three ways: yes, no, and not yet. So, whatever your answer is, Lord, we ask you to give us the strength to accept. Help us to do what is right and just. In Jesus, Our Lord and Redeemer's name, we pray. Amen.

Romans 1:9: "For God is my witness, whom I serve with my spirit in the gospel of his Son, that without ceasing I make mention of you always in my prayers."

Printed in the United States
By Bookmasters